vanishing from
FORESTS
&Jungles

by Gail Radley

illustrations by Jean Sherlock

Featuring poems by Jack Prelutsky, William Blake, and others

Carolrhoda Books, Inc./Minneapolis

"Be infinitely tender and loving to animals." —'Abdu'l-Baha
For my dear friends the Neiheisels—Robin, Bill, Lauren, and especially Philip—because they care.

The status of animals can change over time. To find out about an animal's current status, you can check this website: **<http://endangered.fws.gov/wildlife.html#species>**. For animals outside the United States, click on "Species Listed in Other Countries."

Photos in this book are used courtesy of: p. 4, © Edward Parker; p. 5, Gerald and Buff Corsi/Focus on Nature, Inc.

Text copyright © 2001 by Gail Radley
Illustrations copyright © 2001 by Jean Sherlock

This book is available in two editions:
Library binding by Carolrhoda Books, Inc.,
    a division of Lerner Publishing Group
Soft cover by First Avenue Editions,
    an imprint of Lerner Publishing Group
241 First Avenue North
Minneapolis, Minnesota 55401 U.S.A.

Website address: www.lernerbooks.com

Words in **bold type** are explained in a glossary on page 30.

Library of Congress Cataloging-in-Publication Data
Radley, Gail.
    Forests and jungles / by Gail Radley; illustrations by Jean Sherlock.
        p. cm. — (Vanishing from)
    Includes index.
    Summary: Through short essays and poems, discusses ten endangered species that live in forests or jungles, including scientific information about each, reasons for its endangered status, and descriptions of efforts to protect it.
    ISBN 1-57505-405-1 (lib. bdg. : alk. paper) ISBN 1-57505-567-8 (pbk.)
    1. Forest animals—Juvenile literature. 2. Jungle animals—Juvenile literature.
3. Endangered species—Juvenile literature. [1. Forest animals. 2. Jungle animals. 3. Endangered species.] I. Sherlock, Jean, ill. II. Title. III. Series: Radley, Gail. Vanishing from.
QL112.R34 2001
591.73—dc21   97-27614

Manufactured in the United States of America
1 2 3 4 5 6 – JR – 06 05 04 03 02 01

Contents

Introduction

What would you do if the very last giant panda on earth was dying? You'd probably try to save it. Animals are dying out far more often than you might think. Scientists believe that about 50 **species,** or kinds, of animals die out each day. What's going on?

To understand, it might help to imagine all the pieces of a big jigsaw puzzle. Some pieces don't look important, and it's hard to see how they fit. But would you throw away those pieces? Of course not! You need them all to make a complete picture.

A giant elephant and a small white bird called a cattle egret help one another survive. The cattle egret eats insects on the elephant's skin. Besides grooming the elephant, the egret also acts as an alarm system, warning the elephant of approaching danger.

Our planet is a lot like a huge puzzle. The pieces come in different sizes. Some forms of life, such as bacteria, are very tiny. Others, like the mighty elephant or the towering redwood tree, are hard to miss.

Like puzzle pieces, all the living and nonliving things on the earth are connected. Some of the most important pieces of the puzzle combine to make up **habitats.** A habitat is the place where a plant or animal naturally lives. A habitat is made up of a mix of soil, air, water, weather, and living **organisms.**

The organisms in a habitat depend on each other to live. An **ecosystem** is the combination of organisms and their habitat. All ecosystems undergo change over time. Throughout history, changes in climate or habitat have made it more difficult for animals in an ecosystem to survive. When an ecosystem changes slowly, species have time to adapt. They can develop new traits to help them survive.

However, humans put many species in danger by making quicker changes to habitats. We cut down trees or grass so we can grow food or build houses. Humans also change environments by bringing in new plants and animals. The new species may compete with native species for food and space.

Humans use large amounts of natural resources. Water shortages and soil contamination change animal habitats. Hunting by humans has caused some species to die out and has pushed others in that direction. Laws to protect animals don't always help. Some animals have hides or other parts that are worth a lot of money. **Poachers**—people who hunt illegally—kill animals that are protected by law and sell their parts.

When the last member of an animal species dies, the species is **extinct.** Every animal that becomes extinct is a piece of the puzzle lost. And once that piece is gone, it's gone forever.

What's Being Done?

Scientists carefully watch animal populations. They call a species that's likely to become extinct **endangered.** **Threatened** creatures are not yet endangered, but their populations are shrinking. Some species fit into the **rare** category, meaning there have never been many of these creatures. A drop in a rare animal's population can push those creatures into the threatened group.

Ecologists make a recovery plan for animals in danger. They look at each creature's needs and think of ways to help meet those needs. Ecologists might suggest that lawmakers limit hunting of certain species. Sometimes scientists start a captive-breeding program. Wildlife experts capture threatened or endangered animals and take them to a zoo or a wildlife research center. Scientists hope the animals will be able to have babies and raise them in these safe places. If scientists believe the animals can survive in the wild, they may release some back into their natural habitat.

Scientists might recommend that land be set aside for a **wildlife refuge.** Here they maintain or restore habitats so that the land will support endangered, threatened, or rare creatures.

What Can You Do?

In *Forests & Jungles,* you'll take a close look at 10 species in danger. As you read about these animals, think about how their stories make you feel. Do you feel sad? Or angry? Or happy that a species is doing better? A lot of people have written poems or essays to express their feelings about animals in danger. In this book, you will find a poem or another writing about each animal.

Reading about so many threatened animals can be overwhelming. You might think, "What could I possibly do that would make any difference?" Think again! Remember that big changes have to start somewhere. And they usually begin with small steps. To learn about what you can do to help, see the What You Can Do section on page 29.

KEY **FACTS**

STATUS:
Endangered

SCIENTIFIC NAME:
*Ailuropoda
melanoleuca*

HISTORIC RANGE:
China

SIZE:
5 to 6 feet tall;
weighs up to
400 pounds

DIET:
Mainly bamboo;
also some types
of flowers, fish,
and small rodents

LIFE SPAN:
26+ years
(in captivity)

GIANT Panda

Giant pandas look like teddy bears. They are furry and black and white. Their natural habitat is the bamboo forests of western and southwestern China. Giant pandas eat mainly bamboo plants. But the bamboo plants are not very nutritious. So giant pandas have to eat a lot of bamboo. They usually eat for more than 10 hours each day.

Pandas rely on bamboo forests for food. Without bamboo, the animals cannot survive. Chinese people have cut down much of the bamboo forests. On the cleared land, they have built farms and homes.

Another problem is that bamboo plants are slow to reproduce. They only grow seeds once— when the plant is 10 to 120 years old. After a bamboo plant produces seeds, it dies.

Only about 1,000 giant pandas still live in the wild. The Chinese government has set aside places called **preserves.** In the preserves, giant pandas can live in safety.

Bei-shung

I am Bei-shung, they call me the white bear.
I am the hidden king of these bamboo forests,
Invisible with my white fur and my black fur
Among this snow, these dark rocks and shadows.

I am the hidden king of these mountain heights,
Not a clown, not a toy. I do not care
To be seen. I walk, for all my weight,
Like a ghost on the soles of my black feet.

Invisible with my black fur and my white fur
I haunt the streams. I flip out little fishes;
I scoop them out of the water with my hand.
(I have a thumb, like you. I have a hand.)

Among this sparkling snow, these rocks and shadows,
I roam. Time is my own. My teeth are massive.
My jaw is a powerful grinder. I feed
On chewy bamboo, on small creatures, fish, birds.

You call me Panda. I am King Bei-shung.

— Gerard Benson

KEY *FACTS*

STATUS:
Endangered

SCIENTIFIC NAME:
*Gymnobelideus
leadbeateri*

HISTORIC RANGE:
Victoria and
New South Wales
(Australian
states)

SIZE:
13 to 13¾ inches
long, including a
7-inch tail; weighs
2 to 4 ounces

DIET:
Eucalyptus nectar
and pollen, fruits,
and insects

LIFE SPAN:
May live more
than 9 years

LEADBEATER'S
Possum

A possum is a small, furry animal with paws that look like hands. Possums are marsupials. Marsupials carry their young in pouches on their bellies. The Leadbeater's possum has gray-brown fur and lives in the forests of southeastern Australia.

Like other possums, Leadbeater's possums sleep during the day and eat at night. Groups of eight or more share nests in eucalyptus trees. The possum's hooked claws allow it to easily grab on to branches. The possum uses its tail for balance as it jumps from branch to branch.

The forests where the Leadbeater's possum lives are disappearing quickly. Wood used for building and making paper products is needed. So logging companies have begun cutting down the trees where the possums nest. Without places to nest, possums are more vulnerable to predators.

Environmentalists are working to help the possum survive. But logging continues to threaten the creature's habitat.

Sleep, Possums

Sleep, possums,
The sun is rising;
Hide away in leafy hollow,
In snuggled warmth.
Hide away, hide away,
Dream of leaping branch to branch,
Acrobats amongst the gum leaves.
Dream of sweet, flowered forests
And the sheltering night.

Sleep, possums.
The sun is rising.

— Gail Radley

TASMANIAN Forester Kangaroo

KEY FACTS

STATUS:
Endangered

SCIENTIFIC NAME:
Macropus giganteus tasmaniensis

HISTORIC RANGE:
Tasmania (an island state of Australia)

SIZE:
Up to 6 feet tall; weighs up to 200 pounds

DIET:
Mainly grass

LIFE SPAN:
17 to 18 years (in captivity)

Tasmanian forester kangaroos live in Tasmania, an island near Australia. The kangaroos live in small groups, usually consisting of a mother and her babies. They rest in the shade during the day. At night they graze on grass and small plants.

For hundreds of years, people have hunted Tasmanian forester kangaroos for their hides and meat. Ranchers have also hunted the animals. Many kangaroos live on or near ranch land. The kangaroos damage fences and compete with sheep for grazing land. Tasmania has more mountains than grassland for grazing. Ranchers killed the kangaroos to protect their pastureland.

By the early 1900s, the number of kangaroos had dropped severely. Building new homes has damaged the kangaroo's habitat, too. Hunters continue to kill the animals even though they are endangered. But because most Tasmanian forester kangaroos live on private land, it is hard for environmental groups to protect them.

Kangaroo

In the forest clearing
Beneath the pine and eucalyptus tree
A kangaroo mother rests in the midday sun
With her baby, her joey, warmly tucked in her pouch
Mouth dripping with milk, snugly hidden away—
Yet faraway hearing
Alert, joey, ever listening
To so faintly the distance—
The shriek pierce of wild dogs
Hungry for prey.

— Jill Morgan Hawkins

13

KEY *FACTS*

STATUS:
Endangered

SCIENTIFIC NAME:
Achatinella spp.
(all species)

HISTORIC RANGE:
Oahu (a Hawaiian island)

SIZE:
Shell length of
$1/2$ inch to slightly
over 1 inch

DIET:
Fungi and algae

LIFE SPAN:
20 years or more

OAHU
Tree Snail

Oahu tree snails cling to tree branches on the Hawaiian island of Oahu. They also nestle in leaves on the ground. Many snails live their entire lives on one tree.

An Oahu tree snail cannot have babies until it is six or seven years old. Then a tree snail has one baby at a time. If snails do not live long enough to have babies, the snail population can fall sharply.

More and more often, snails do not live to be six years old. Many of the trees on Oahu have been cut down. Pastures, farms, and homes replace the trees. Trees from other parts of the world are quick to grow where others have been cut down. But the snail cannot live on those trees.

The Oahu tree snail is also threatened by a snail that feeds on other snails. The government brought in a snail from Florida to protect Oahu's fields from crop-eating snails. But the Florida snail also eats tree snails. Shell collectors put the snail at risk, too. The Oahu tree snail's colorful shell is easy to spot. Away from its habitat, the snail cannot survive for long.

The night was hot . . .
    stripped to the waist
    the snail
enjoyed the moonlight

— *Issa*

TIMBER Wolf

KEY FACTS

STATUS:
Varies by U.S. state (status under review)

SCIENTIFIC NAME:
Canis lupus

HISTORIC RANGE:
Northern Hemisphere

SIZE:
Up to 2½ feet tall at shoulder; weighs up to 120 pounds

DIET:
Mainly large, hoofed animals

LIFE SPAN:
16 years or more

The saying "lone wolf" describes someone who likes to be alone. But most timber wolves travel in family packs. Wolves even "talk" to each other by howling.

The timber wolf is a type of gray wolf that lives in wooded areas all over the United States. Timber wolves hunt bison, deer, elk, and moose for food. Early U.S. settlers hunted the same animals. They killed off much of the wolves' food. So timber wolves turned to cattle and sheep. Ranchers hired hunters to kill the wolves. By the early 1900s, timber wolves were in danger of disappearing for good.

The U.S. Endangered Species Act of 1973 limited hunting. The act also protected certain kinds of wildlife habitats. Under this act, wolf populations grew in Minnesota and Michigan. In the mid-1990s, the U.S. government moved about 60 timber wolves from Canada into Idaho, Montana, and Wyoming. The government agreed to pay ranchers for lost livestock. These efforts seem to be restoring the population of the timber wolf.

The Wolf

When the pale moon hides and the wind wails,
And over the tree-tops the nighthawk sails,
The gray wolf sits on the world's far rim,
And howls: and it seems to comfort him.

The wolf is a lonely soul, you see,
No beast in the wood, nor bird in the tree,
But shuns his path; in the windy gloom
They give him plenty, and plenty of room.

So he sits with his long, lean face to the sky
Watching the ragged clouds go by.
There in the night, alone, apart,
Singing the song of his lone, wild heart.

Far away, on the world's dark rim
He howls, and it seems to comfort him.

— **Georgia Roberts Durston**

KEY *FACTS*

STATUS:
Endangered

SCIENTIFIC NAME:
Bradypus torquatus

HISTORIC RANGE:
Brazil

SIZE:
Up to 2 feet long, including tail; weighs up to 11 pounds

DIET:
Leaves, flowers, fruits, shoots

LIFE SPAN:
Up to 30 years

BRAZILIAN
Three-toed Sloth

The Brazilian three-toed sloth lives life upside down! The sloth's long, curved claws allow it to cling to branches. Sloths eat, sleep, mate, give birth, and care for their babies in trees. Sloths sleep 15 to 18 hours a day.

Snakes, birds, jaguars, ocelots, and humans all hunt the sloth. Hunters like its flavorful meat. People turn the animal's fur into saddlecloths. They string sloth claws onto necklaces. Because the sloth moves so slowly, its best hope is to blend in with the trees. The greenish algae that grow in the sloth's fur help it hide.

The destruction of the Amazon **tropical rain forest,** where the Brazilian three-toed sloth lives, puts the creature in great danger. People cut down the trees to make room for farms. In Brazil, the government has passed laws that ban logging in some areas of the Amazon rain forest. But the sloth remains endangered.

The Three-toed Sloth

The three-toed sloth is in a deep
and curious and wakeless sleep.
The boughs and branches bend and break,
but seldom does the sloth awake.
The noisy jungle far below
is not for three-toed sloths to know.

— Jack Prelutsky

Gorilla

KEY *FACTS*

STATUS:
Endangered

SCIENTIFIC NAME:
Gorilla gorilla

HISTORIC RANGE:
Central and
western Africa

SIZE:
Up to 6 feet tall;
weighs up to
450 pounds

DIET:
Bark, buds,
fruits, and leaves

LIFE SPAN:
Up to 50 years
(in captivity)

Even though gorillas look big and scary, they are shy and usually quiet. Gorillas travel in groups of 2 to 30. Gorilla groups follow the lead of an older male and act like a family. A group spends the day searching for food. By midmorning, the older members rest. The young gorillas wrestle, swing from vines, and play games.

In the Congo River Basin of central Africa, fewer and fewer gorillas can be found. Loss of habitat is one of the reasons. But hunting is another threat. Poachers make a lot of money by selling body parts as souvenirs. People also capture young gorillas for zoos. When female gorillas try to protect their young, people sometimes kill them.

National parks in central Africa give gorillas a safe place to live. Fees from park tourists help replace the money that was once earned from gorilla hunting. But civil wars rage in several African countries. Soldiers do not pay attention to national park boundaries while at war. Many efforts to help gorillas have stopped.

Gorilla

Hairy arms, egg-shaped head;
Fierce appearance, but a gentle heart.
His shifty old eyes slide intelligently,
Searching the terrain.
As he eats his lower jaw rotates,
With a munch and a crunch he consumes his food.

His massive muscular body crouches tightly on the ground.
Heavily, clumsily, he swings through the trees,
He drops to the ground;
His arms are crutches—his body sways between them.
His legs are lazy and rarely used.

He scrambles behind wild bushes,
Then rustles,
Then, with a crash, he's gone.

— Class 4S, Simon Marks Primary School

KEY *FACTS*

STATUS:
Endangered

SCIENTIFIC NAME:
*Sciurus niger
cinereus*

HISTORIC RANGE:
Delaware,
Maryland, and
Virginia to
southeastern
Pennsylvania

SIZE:
Up to $10^{3}/_{4}$ inches
long, including
tail; weighs 18
to 46 ounces

DIET:
Nuts, tree buds,
flowers, fungi,
insects, fruits,
and bird eggs

LIFE SPAN:
Up to 9 years
(in captivity)

DELMARVA PENINSULA
Fox Squirrel

Squirrels seem plentiful. You might see them darting around forests, parks, and backyards. But several types of squirrels, including the Delmarva Peninsula fox squirrel, are endangered. The Delmarva, one of the smaller fox squirrels, likes older forests near streams and grasslands. This kind of habitat was once found all over Pennsylvania, New Jersey, Delaware, Maryland, and Virginia. But the Delmarva's habitat has become quite rare.

In the past, hunters killed this squirrel for its tasty meat. In modern times, people have cleared forests for farming and housing. As the fox squirrel's habitat has disappeared, so has the animal.

By the early 1900s, this fox squirrel had vanished from Pennsylvania, New Jersey, Delaware, and most of Virginia. In the 1980s, scientists moved some of Maryland's squirrels back to the states where they had disappeared. This effort helped the Delmarva Peninsula fox squirrel population grow. But the squirrel remains endangered.

Where Is It?

He flips his tail
  And points his nose
And digs it up
  With frantic claws—
That nut he buried
  Long ago
When there wasn't
  Any snow.

He holds it tight
  Between his paws,
Cracks it with
  His little jaws,
And eats it up,
  Then off he goes . . .

But how is he sure a nut's still there?
And how can he guess exactly where?
Squirrel never needs to guess.
He knows.

— **Dorothy Aldis**

23

KEY *FACTS*

STATUS:
Threatened

SCIENTIFIC NAME:
*Loxodonta
africana*

HISTORIC RANGE:
Africa, south of
the Sahara

SIZE:
10 to 13 feet tall
at the shoulder;
weighs up to
15,000 pounds

DIET:
Grass, leaves,
twigs, bark,
and fruits

LIFE SPAN:
Up to 60 years

AFRICAN
Elephant

African elephants live south of the Sahara Desert in Africa. They roam through forests, grasslands, mountains, swamps, and shrub areas. Poachers are the greatest threat to the African elephant. They have killed thousands of elephants for their tusks. The ivory tusks on either side of the trunk can grow from 6 to 8 feet long and weigh as much as 100 pounds. The tusks are carved into billiard balls, piano keys, and trinkets.

During the 1980s, hunting cut the number of African elephants in half. In 1989 many concerned nations banned the trading of ivory. Hunting elephants was outlawed. Some African nations set aside land as elephant preserves. It is against the law to hunt elephants on the preserves.

The ban has helped the elephant population start to recover. In 1997 conservationists decided to allow nations with fast-growing elephant populations to sell some ivory.

I had seen a herd of elephant traveling through dense native forest . . . pacing along as if they had an appointment at the end of the world.

— Isak Dinesen

BENGAL Tiger

KEY FACTS

STATUS:
Endangered

SCIENTIFIC NAME:
Panthera tigris tigris

HISTORIC RANGE:
Temperate and tropical Asia

SIZE:
Up to 9½ feet long; weighs up to 420 pounds

DIET:
Deer, wild boar, antelope, monkeys, and other animals

LIFE SPAN:
Up to 20 years

The Bengal tiger is one of the fastest-disappearing animals in the world. The tigers live in southern Asia. Each Bengal tiger lives and hunts within a 25- to 250-square-mile area. But people have cut down the tiger's forests for cropland. When the tiger's food becomes scarce, the swift and powerful cat sometimes attacks humans.

Between 1975 and 1987, Bengal tigers killed about 600 people in India. The Indian government launched Operation Tiger. This program set up tiger preserves. The preserves keep both the tigers and the villagers safe.

A **buffer zone** surrounds each preserve. In these areas, tigers can hunt animals. Villagers can fish or gather honey, wood, and grass in buffer zones, too. An even safer **mixed-use zone** surrounds the buffer zone. It provides trees for logging and land for livestock. Operation Tiger has helped the tiger population begin to recover.

From *The Tiger*

Tiger! Tiger! Burning bright
In the forests of the night,
What immortal hand or eye
Could frame thy fearful symmetry?

In what distant deeps or skies
Burnt the fire of thine eyes?
On what wings dare he aspire?
What the hand dare seize the fire?

And what shoulder, and what art,
Could twist the sinews of thy heart?
And when thy heart began to beat,
What dread hand? and what dread feet? . . .

Tiger! Tiger! Burning bright
In the forests of the night,
What immortal hand or eye
Dare frame thy fearful symmetry?

— William Blake

Map of Animal Ranges

Hawaii (U.S.)

NORTH AMERICA

SOUTH AMERICA

EUROPE

ASIA

AFRICA

AUSTRALIA

- Giant panda
- Tasmanian forester kangaroo
- Three-toed sloth
- African elephant
- Oahu tree snail
- Leadbeater's possum
- Timber wolf
- Gorilla
- Bengal tiger
- Delmarva Peninsula fox squirrel

What You Can Do

The problem of species in danger may seem too big to tackle. But the efforts of many concerned people have saved some creatures from extinction. There are lots of things that young people can do to help.

Educate yourself.

- *Read books, nature magazines, and newspaper articles to learn about the animals. Then share your knowledge. When you spread the word about an animal in danger, you'll find that other people may want to help.*

- *Discuss a book about endangered animals for your next book report.*

- *Create a class scrapbook with pictures of each student's favorite endangered species.*

- *Create a save-the-animals bulletin board at school.*

- *Make informative buttons to wear on clothes or backpacks.*

- *Ask your teacher to arrange for a local conservationist to talk to your class.*

Take action.

- *Join a conservation club. People in these groups work to educate the public about endangered animals and their habitats.*

- *Encourage people not to buy products made from wild animal parts.*

- *When your parents are buying furniture or other products, ask if they'll shop around until they find ecosystem-friendly items.*

Help animals before they become threatened or endangered.

- *Set up a feeder for migratory birds.*

- *Help reduce air pollution—bike, walk, bus, or carpool.*

- *Pitch in on local clean-up days and encourage people not to litter.*

Decrease the amount of garbage your family or school produces.

- *Recycle glass, metal, paper, and plastic.*

- *Buy products made from recycled materials and shop at secondhand stores.*

- *"Precycle"—buy products that use the least packaging, such as food in bulk bins.*

For More Information

The following organizations have more tips on what you can do to help endangered wildlife:

National Audubon Society, 700 Broadway • New York, NY 10003 www.audubon.org

National Wildlife Federation, 8925 Leesburg Pike • Vienna, VA 22184 www.nwf.org

Sierra Club, 85 Second Street, Second Floor • San Francisco, CA 94105 www.sierraclub.org

World Wildlife Fund/Conservation Foundation, Education Department • 1250 24th Street NW • Washington, D.C. 20037 www.worldwildlife.org

Glossary

buffer zone: land set aside to separate wild animals from people to keep both safe

ecosystem: a carefully balanced community of soil, air, water, climate, and organisms

endangered: a category used by conservationists to describe species that are in danger of becoming extinct and that are unlikely to survive if present conditions continue

extinct: no longer existing

habitat: the place or environment where a plant or animal naturally lives

mixed-use zone: an area in which more than one type of activity is allowed

organism: any living thing

poacher: a person who illegally hunts wildlife

preserve: land set aside for the preservation of an animal or plant species

rare: a category used by conservationists to describe species with small but stable populations that require careful watching

species: the basic groups into which scientists classify animals. Animals in the same species share traits that make them different from all other life-forms.

threatened: a category used by conservationists to describe species that are in danger of becoming extinct, but to a lesser degree than those that are described as endangered

tropical rain forest: a thick evergreen forest that grows in the hot, wet zone around the earth's equator between the Tropic of Cancer and the Tropic of Capricorn

wildlife refuge: land set aside as a shelter where wildlife can safely live

Further Reading

Cerfolli, Fulvio. *Adapting to the Environment.* Austin, TX: Raintree Steck-Vaughn, 1999.

Gallant, Roy A. *Earth's Vanishing Forests.* New York: Macmillan Publishing, 1992.

Greenaway, Theresa. *Jungle.* London: Dorling Kindersley Ltd., 1994.

Harrison, Michael, and Christopher Stuart-Clark. *Oxford Book of Animal Poems.* New York: Oxford University Press, 1992.

Mutel, Cornelia F., and Mary M. Rodgers. *Our Endangered Planet: Tropical Rain Forests.* Minneapolis: Lerner Publications Company, 1991.

Patent, Dorothy Hinshaw. *Children Save the Rain Forest.* New York: Cobblehill Books, 1996.

Vergoth, Karin, and Christopher Lampton. *Endangered Species.* New York: Franklin Watts, 1999.

Index   Numbers in **bold** refer to illustrations

About the Author and Illustrator

Gail Radley has published almost two dozen books. An animal lover, she's concerned about the large number of species whose survival is in danger. Radley lives with her husband, Joe, daughter, Jana, and their schnauzer, Toby, in DeLand, Florida. She is a lecturer in the English department at Stetson University.

Illustrator Jean Sherlock has long been combining her love of wildlife and her artistic talents. Her nature illustrations first appeared in publications while she was still in her early teens. When Jean isn't behind her easel, her interests include fishing, bird-watching, and above all, falconry. She and her red-tailed hawk enjoy hunting excursions throughout the United States.

Poetry Acknowledgments

The poems included in *Forests & Jungles* are reprinted with the permission of the following: p. 9 "Beishung," first published by Penguin, London, is included by permission of the author, Gerard Benson (of *Poems on the Underground*); p. 11 "Sleep, Possums" by Gail Radley; p. 13 "Kangaroo," printed by permission of Jill Morgan Hawkins; p. 15 "The night was hot . . ." Copyright © by 1958 Peter Pauper Press. Translation by Peter Beilenson. Reprinted by permission; p. 17 "The Wolf," the author has made every effort to obtain permission to use "The Wolf" by Georgia Roberts Durston; p. 19 "The Three-toed Sloth" by Jack Prelutsky, reprinted by permission of Greenwillow Books, a division of William Morrow and Co., Inc. Copyright © 1983 by Jack Prelutsky; p. 21 "Gorilla," the author has made every effort to obtain permission to use "Gorilla" by Class 4S, Simon Marks Primary School; p. 23 "Where Is It?" by Dorothy Aldis, reprinted by permission of G. P. Putnam's Sons from *Is Anybody Hungry?* Copyright © 1964 by Dorothy Aldis; p. 25 (prose excerpt) "I had seen a herd of elephant traveling through" from *Out of Africa* by Isak Dinesen. Copyright © 1937 by Random House, Inc. Copyright renewed 1965 by Rungstedlundfonden. Reprinted by permission of Random House, Inc.; p. 27 excerpted from "The Tiger" (in the public domain) by William Blake.